Australian Shepherd Puppy Training

The Complete Guide with the Essential Techniques for Raising and Training Your Aussie without Mistakes.

By

Polly Saunders

Table of Contents

Introduction

Australian Shepherds have a ton of qualities to offer. They are loyal, have unlimited energy, give infinite love, and are sweet and affectionate life companions. They are so charming that no person would not want at least one as a family member.

This guide contains all the necessary information easy to follow and valuable for initial training. If you are about to buy your Australian Shepherd puppy, purchase this guide so that you can prepare yourself quickly and effectively to enter this beautiful furry creature into your life. This guide can be handy even if you already have an adult dog or another puppy at home.

Training to welcome an Australian Shepherd puppy requires considerable efforts, but your dog will pay them all back as soon as he enters the house. Indeed, you are getting a puppy because you and your family enjoy their company; for this, enjoy every phase of your training, living it in a carefree and cheerful way.

To keep you carefree and the book light, I've added some funny stories about my dog so you can get a healthy dose of humor and fun. Dogs are fun and caring, and they are often excellent listeners, thus serving as therapists.

Studying this guide well will allow you to be prepared when you first hug him upon his arrival. This will help your puppy feel right at home and will help you establish the right mindset for training and raising an Australian Shepherd puppy.

Within this guide, you will find information that will be useful for you to correctly choose and understand everything you need to raise an Australian Shepherd wisely. You will learn to live with a happy, calm, and polite partner.

Through this book, you will understand well the characteristics and peculiarities of this beautiful breed. You can take all the fundamental steps to train an Australian Shepherd.

Having an Australian shepherd at home is a commitment that requires patience, application, and altruism. But you don't have to think it's a game! Before looking for the puppy you want from a breeder, you must have studied and been prepared for what awaits you.

Although Australian Shepherds are now bred as companion dogs, this was not the goal of the first Australian breeders who wanted a strong and resilient dog that could look after their livestock for days on end.

So, the reasons a person decides to get an Australian Shepherd have changed over time, but the disposition of dogs has not. They are always extraordinary animals dedicated to working and with deep thrusts to the care and surveillance of the herd. If he has no cattle nearby, the Australian Shepherd will look after the children or smaller dogs he has on hand with the same love.

The Australian Shepherd can give you a lot of energy and love. But, to make him feel good, you will have to work hard to ensure him a suitable space to move, and you will have to have a lot of patience and attention to help him grow happy.

If you feel you are the right person to raise an Australian Shepherd puppy and believe the Australian Shepherd is right for you, study this guide thoroughly.

CHAPTER 1: Biography and general characteristics of the Australian Shepherd

1.1 Introductory remarks

Suppose you have just gotten an Australian Shepherd or are about to do so. In that case, you need to learn some basics about this beautiful breed to understand how to train and educate your Australian Shepherd properly.

Then, you will enter a fantastic world and discover how wonderful to have him beside you as a best friend.

These dogs are called shepherds because they were initially bred to protect and raise cattle or sheep. The breed originates in the western United States, where breeders have worked for many years to train the shepherd dog par excellence. However, the reason they are called Australians lies in the fact that the first owners of these dogs came from Australia.

Australian Shepherds are famous for their varied colors, and they have uniform and showy coats with beautiful curls.

You can find them in full red, red merle, entirely black, and blue merle, and there are two-tone and tricolor combinations based on the range of colors. Each color type may have white markings or copper spots on the chest, face, and legs.

Their weight varies from 35 to 70 kilos, and their tails can be tall and thin or long and full. During the spring, Australian Shepherds mutate, preparing for the hot summer season. This aspect you must consider before buying it because if you can't stand finding dog hair all over the house, the Australian Shepherd may not be for you.

In addition, they tend to be very reserved, and in some cases, they could even be aggressive towards strangers, having an innate nature as a guard dog.

Therefore, they are intelligent dogs, easy to train, loyal, affectionate, and friendly to the people they love. If they are raised correctly, they are protective of children and other puppies. They love playing and working outdoors and are reasonable and kind pastoral dogs. The Australian Shepherd is probably the easiest dog to train.

You can leave them indoors safely, but remember that they still need many hours outdoors to play and exercise. It would be a great idea to reserve a yard or garden for your Australian Shepherd.

If you are away from home all day, this is probably not the right dog for you; if left on their own for a long time, Australian Shepherds may develop separation anxiety.

1.2 History and origin of the Australian Shepherd

Understanding the origins and history of the Australian Shepherd is no easy task. This breed, as mentioned above, originated in the western United States, where they were bred and raised as hardy and hardworking herding dogs.

They have been mixed with German, British, and Scottish shepherd breeds (such as the Border Collie) in these areas. The breeders did not care about the dogs' physical appearance but only about their performance.

Australian Shepherds were in high demand because they could adapt quickly to the climate of high altitudes, particularly the extreme environment of the Rocky Mountains. Another feature much appreciated by breeders was the excellent eyesight that allowed them to carry out search and rescue operations for livestock and the herding animals and poultry. They are very agile animals, therefore perfect for outdoor work and canine agility sports, and they have a highly developed sense of smell.

They are obedient and devoted dogs, all fundamental qualities for dynamic and strenuous activities. They are famous for the strange coat colors, which are the main hallmark of the breed.

The word "Australian" is misused because these dogs are not native to Australia. He was originally called a **Spanish Shepherd**, **Austrian Shepherd**, **Californian Shepherd**, and **New Mexican Shepherd**. The reason why he was named the Australian Shepherd is explained by the fact that many breeders came from Australia.

In the United States, Australian Shepherds are in the top 20 most common breeds, which is very simple. They are fantastic dogs, devoted to their owners and eager to make them happy.

You will love your Australian Shepherd because he will work hard to help you and always obey you, and love your attention.

1.2.1 The pastoral spirit of the Aussie

You will be utterly amazed by the herding spirit that your Aussie embodies.

His pastoral side derives from his history and the lifestyle he has had since the beginning. This dog is happy and comfortable in a vast field of sheep or cattle. Yet, he must protect and feel useful for the work he has been entrusted with.

You could be deceived by the name, imagining a dog engaged in the harsh work of the hinterland, which may bark with a solid Australian accent. But, as soon as you see your Aussie for the first time, it will feel like you know a sheepskin rug being pulled from under your feet.

1.3 Teamwork with men

Dogs and people are a great team. Each party has guaranteed protection and safety to the other party, always working together. Over the years, specific breeds of dogs have developed and grown to perform particular tasks and roles within this team.

Some dog breeds have a robust structure to support their bark and an innate instinct for protection and defense. For these characteristics, they have been bred specifically to protect people and livestock from any attack by predators.

Other dog breeds are very fast and agile and are used to herd livestock and prevent an animal from straying from the herd. Additional dog breeds have both characteristics and are given tasks such as retrieving and hunting.

The qualities and strengths described so far have evolved. Humans have always carefully bred various dog breeds to meet their needs, thus developing an intense and boundless relationship with them.

In North America, European settlers not only came with their families but also with their cattle and dogs to breed on the vast plains that existed.

Therefore, men and dogs came from all parts of Europe, mixed with the breeds already in the area. Here's how new crosses and breeds mixed and evolved in North America.

1.4 How did the Australian Shepherd become known?

We still don't know how the Australian Shepherd became known, although we know a lot about this fantastic dog. There are several theories on this subject, but none have been universally accepted.

It, therefore, remains a mystery, which contributes to increasing the charm of the Australian Shepherd.

According to one theory, the ancestors of today's dogs came from Basque shepherds coming directly from Australia.

However, it is not very reliable as a theory as almost all Basque shepherds who came to North America in the late nineteenth century were from the **Basque Country of Spain** and **France** or **South America**. Furthermore, even before these migrations, dogs were known as Australian Shepherds.

The dogs that accompanied the Basque Shepherds did not have some of the most common traits of the Australian Shepherd, the bluish-gray color and the mottled black coat. Instead, the origins of this breed can be traced through color, a fascinating shade known as "**merle**."

1.5 When the Aussie became a breed

The Australian Shepherd remained quiet about his duties on the ranches until the mid-twentieth century, when they became rodeo stars. Then, thanks to his intelligence and speed, the Australian was taken on a tour where he dazzled the crowd with his athleticism and agility.

Subsequently, the world of Hollywood noticed this splendid dog and made him the protagonist in many cinema classics.

Naturally, as soon as people saw these dogs in action, they fell in love with them and began to travel from one part of the country to the other to see their performances and take them home.

During these years, the Australian Shepherd became very well-known and, above all, began to be sought after by many people.

1.5.1 Formation of the Australian Shepherd Club of America (ASCA)

The rise of the Aussie was very rapid, so much so that in 1957 the Australian Shepherd Club of America (**ASCA**) was created, making it even more famous and popular.

Towards the end of the 1960s, the number of Australian Shepherd owners who wanted to exhibit their dogs at events, fairs, and herding competitions increased. After about ten years, in the late 1970s, an official breed standard was assigned to the Australian Shepherd.

But there was still a problem. **The American Kennel Club** (**AKC**) had not yet declared the Australian Shepherd an official breed, even though the Aussie had become very popular.

So, when this appointment was first proposed in the mid-1980s, it was rejected because the species would be divided into a shepherd dog and a show dog.

The breeders feared that the Australian Shepherd would become even more known and sought after, especially by people who only wanted to have him as a pet. In reality, even if criticized by public opinion, breeders cared about the well-being and health of the dog.

In addition to being intelligent and loyal, Australian Shepherds have a docile nature that allows them to be fantastic pets. Still, at the same time, they are fatigue dogs to which not everyone can guarantee what they need.

The race was not divided but human beings, with the creation of a group, the **United States Australian Shepherd Association** (**USASA**), by those who wanted at all costs to recognize the Aussie as a dog breed. Finally, complete and shared recognition was granted by the **Australian Kennel Club** (AKC) in the early 1990s.

The Australian Shepherd has fascinated dog lovers for many years by winning prizes at dog shows and successfully overcoming demanding herding competitions. But not only!

Homelife with an Australian Shepherd is beautiful and if you want to become the perfect owner of an Aussie, read the following few chapters carefully.

CHAPTER 2: What you need to know to train Australian Shepherd puppies

You will be able to raise an educated dog if you can take the time to teach him the basic rules that he must respect and the limits that he must not cross. Teaching him more or less complicated tricks is a great way to see him happy and healthy mentally and physically.

Since he was a puppy, the Australian Shepherd has been a concentrated, intelligent dog, eager to learn and ready to satisfy all the requests of his master effectively. He also has a powerful desire to work.

You need to set aside the time to engage your Australian Shepherd puppy in simple to difficult daily physical and mental exercises; you could have him play canine sports with which your puppy could develop specific skills. You will raise a healthy, happy, physically fit, and active dog.

2.1 Avoids the wrong behaviours

The cause of many of our puppy friends' behavioral problems often comes from humans; this happens most of the time without us even noticing.

If we don't pay attention and calibrate our behaviors well, we could cause our Australian Shepherd puppies many serious problems.

A dog usually bred for hunting, rescue, search, control, and survey work could be unhappy if it is not adequately educated and not involved in dynamic work activities.

To these problems, there could be added other unpleasant situations or events that must be avoided.

2.1.1 The 15 mistakes you must not make

You may inadvertently make mistakes that can harm your puppy for the rest of his life. Listed below are:

1) make him overeat;
2) devote little time to it;
3) do not give him the right energy;
4) don't commit to finding new ways to engage him mentally;
5) do not exercise enough;
6) not knowing the specific needs of your dog's breed;
7) do not accustom your dog to loud noises;
8) be fooled by his sweet eyes to do whatever he asks of you;
9) reward him even when he doesn't deserve it;
10) not learning the notions necessary to raise and educate your dog correctly;
11) become your dog's slave;
12) not to teach him the basic rules and the limits he must not cross;
13) don't give him time to socialize;
14) choose the wrong collar or leash;
15) let your dog sleep in your bed.

These behaviors could make your dog unhappy and could make him physically ill. Do everything to avoid them and create a peaceful environment from the first day your puppy enters your home.

We must also know how to face and overcome the particular adolescent period of a puppy in which we could witness delicate situations and dangerous events. Even if we have good intentions, we can make mistakes by not training or socializing our puppy well through superficiality or lack of attention.

We must be aware that wrong behaviors in this growth phase could have negative consequences for the whole life of our furry friend.

2.2 Socializing your Aussie puppy

In the development and growth of your dog, a fundamental element is your puppy's socialization. This phase begins at birth, and it is your breeder's job to establish effective socialization patterns and strategies with the puppies he raises.

Socialization concerns, in general terms, interaction and relating with others, that is, with adult humans, children, or other dogs. Being social is essential to socialization, but it is not the only one.

Therefore, it is very important to focus not only on one stage of socialization but on the complete socialization of the dog.

You must learn to socialize the dog to a series of stimuli and sensations, thus breeding a healthy dog that is not intimidated by noise. You can help your dog in this fundamental aspect of his life by instilling him with self-confidence, allowing him to relate calmly and serenely to the world around him.

In the following few pages, we'll go over all the proven methods you can use to build the trust your puppy needs.

2.2.1 How to overcome your puppy's behaviour problems

Before you can predict and avoid your Australian Shepherd's most common behavioral issues, you need to understand how directly you can create them inadvertently.

The dog you have chosen will learn to behave directly from you. His actions and habits stem primarily from how he was socialized as a puppy and continued to be socialized over the next few years.

The best and friendliest dog in the world, without proper socialization, could become aggressive, antisocial, neurotic, and could be violent towards other dogs, animals, or people they do not know.

When a dog behaves aggressively in any situation, he will be considered bad or dangerous, depending on how he has been socialized since birth.

2.2.2 How to socialize with unknown humans

To create proper socialization, you must take your puppy with you everywhere and show it to many people of different ages, physical appearances, and ethnicity so he can learn the normal things of everyday life without being stunned by the news he can see.

At the same time, you don't have to take your puppy with you all the time, as he needs to learn on his own and walk on his paws.

If you don't let him go, he may develop unwanted behaviors such as "underarm alligator," which occurs whenever an unknown person greets him; in this situation, your dog may feel in a leadership position where he wants to protect his owner at all costs.

Accustoming your puppy too small children's gestures, unpredictable actions, and noises will be essential. When children play, you need to be vigilant to prevent them from screaming or committing violent actions. It could be not very comforting to an Australian Shepherd puppy who has not yet developed familiarity with human puppies.

You must be especially careful when introducing your Australian Shepherd puppy too small children, as they may unintentionally injure him. You must avoid that your dog is afraid of children, as it could lead to problems of aggression and nastiness in the future; when the puppy grows up, it will attack or bite a child who treats him badly or suddenly invades his space.

As a typical herding dog, the Australian Shepherd could gather children around him by taking them by the ankles. You have to scold your puppy every time he does this, as this behavior is not acceptable.

2.2.3 How to socialize with unfamiliar dogs

A dog that is not properly socialized can be fearful, nervous, and shy, regardless of his personality.

In addition, he may become wary of other dogs, animals, unfamiliar people, or unusual situations and circumstances. All this could generate nervous or unstable behaviors, leading to unacceptable aggression.

One way to immediately make your Australian Shepherd puppy understand the correct behavior is to take him for daily walks on a leash, where he could meet and socialize with other dogs and other people.

When you want to socialize your puppy with other dogs, you must first introduce him to a friendly and calm dog. Training your puppy to be agitated or unfriendly with other dogs would give him a negative experience that could affect him considerably.

He may develop an unmotivated fear of other dogs if he experiences excessively negative experiences at a young age. Therefore, placing the Australian shepherd in a group with at least ten other puppies is advisable so that socialization can be supervised and the games it takes part in can be controlled.

2.2.4 Creation and development of environmental socialization

You don't have to make the mistake of not taking the time to show your Australian Shepherd puppy in a variety of different spaces and environments. Your dog needs to feel comfortable with different sounds, smells, and views because they could develop trauma or stress later in life.

You don't have to take your puppy only to the areas he is used to, i.e., where you live and frequently go. Take it instead to noisy areas, such as airports, construction sites, shopping areas, and crowded places.

2.3 How to overcome the most common fears

2.3.1 Loud and high-pitched noises

Deafening noises such as home security alarms, sirens, thunderstorms, or fireworks can scare your dog. First of all, we as owners must prepare our dogs to face this fear and intervene promptly whenever such a situation occurs.

To do this, you need to work hard to get your dog used to these noises while still young. If you manage to desensitize him, it will be easier for him to resist during holidays like New Year's or Halloween, thunderstorms, or when a police car or ambulance passes by.

Remember that loud and high-pitched noises can damage your dog's sensitive ears; therefore, you must always protect them with your hands when a siren or an alarm starts to blast.

2.3.2 Tools to desensitize your Australian Shepherd

Below you will learn several ways and tools to desensitize and get your Australian Shepherd accustomed to overcoming the fear of loud noises such as alarms and sirens.

Use Radio or TV

It could be helpful to calm your puppy agitated by loud noises to turn on the radio or TV and let him hear relaxing music with a high pitch to cover the noises coming from outside, such as thunder, sirens, or house alarms.

When they hear loud or shrill noises such as alarms, fireworks, or explosions, most dogs get excited and run. In this situation, you will no longer be able to communicate with your puppy because he will behave illogically.

You need to keep your puppy very calm, preventing him from getting injured while running away from these noises.

When he heard the fireworks on New Year's Eve, think that my Australian Shepherd tried to escape through the toilet!

You have to behave well, you don't have to get scared too, and you don't have to appear to your dog sorry, frustrated, or angry. Behavior of this type could only worsen the mood of an agitated dog.

If a dog's owner, who should be his primary support, appears weak or unstable, that dog will feel at a loss because he has no one to get help from. Protect your puppy by pretending nothing has happened and speak to him in a calm but determined voice.

Pop the bubble wrap

Using bubble wrap is a practical and easy way to desensitize your dog from the fear of loud noises and sudden sounds. Show him the bubble wrap, pop a few cells and, if he stays put, give him a prize. Start with a bubble wrap with small, quiet cells and gradually use bubble wrap with large, noisy cells. If your dog reacts well, you can advance the level of exercise by blowing up paper bags or balloons.

Play CDs of unusual sounds

You can buy CDs with collections of sounds such as sirens, fireworks, alarms, clapping, and children's screams in any music shop; you can also create this collection yourself.

Play these CDs for your Australian Shepherd when you work in your study or kitchen and when you relax in the living room or bedroom. You must act as if nothing happened when you play these collections of sounds so that your dog learns not to fidget even when he hears the same noises in other places or other situations.

Have him wear a relaxation collar

You could have your Australian Shepherd puppy wear a specially designed collar to calm and soothe an upset dog. There are two collars of this type: one gives off soothing scents, and another emits shallow and delicate sounds that can calm a frightened dog.

Make him wear a thunder shirt

Another way to calm your dog frightened by sudden noises is by making him wear a thunder shirt, which relieves trauma or anxiety resulting from explosions, rumbles, or loud sounds. The calming effect of the thunder shirt comes from the slight pressure it creates around the dog, almost as if it were a hug.

You should always take time to socialize and desensitize your Australian Shepherd from noisy sounds when they are a puppy and grow up. This will help him not to fidget when he hears a loud and sudden noise, making him calm and peaceful.

You must teach your Australian Shepherd to become a quiet and peaceful family member in every environment and situation.

2.4 Important rules to follow and limits not to be exceeded

You must take the time to teach your Australian Shepherd the basic rules and show him the limits beyond which he must not go. This will help you avoid behavioral problems that will arise in the future. To effectively teach them these fundamentals, you will need to have a calm demeanor, and you will need to be very patient and consistent.

The first rules and limits you need to teach your Australian Shepherd are listed here:

- do not chase the neighbor's cat or other pets;

- do not jump on tables, sofas, counters, or other furniture;

- do not rummage in the garbage can;

- do not damage the cat's litter box, if present in the house;

- do not sleep in the owner's bed;

- do not beg for food at the table while people are eating;

- do not stay in the kitchen while food is being prepared;

- do not bark and do not fidget at every little sound or noise;

- do not go through doors before humans.

Some puppies can start training from 8 weeks, while most will be ready from 12 weeks. If your Australian Shepherd puppy is under 6 weeks of age, you must be careful not to let him do too many activities because his attention span may be limited.

If your puppy is small, train him for a maximum of 10 minutes and create a comfortable and peaceful environment during your training sessions; give him lots of praise and tasty treats so that your puppy is waiting for nothing but the next training session.

Simultaneously with the verbal commands, introduce the signals with your hands so your puppy will recognize them both, being able to replace the verbal commands only with those of the hands in a short time.

Being very intelligent as a breed, the Australian Shepherd will easily understand all the hand signals his owner will give him.

2.5 Always maintain a correct attitude

Your Australian Shepherd can read and understand you like a book, so your attitude must always be transparent. If you are angry with him, he feels it, and if you are in a bad mood or angry for some other reason, he will think your mood depends on him.

During the socialization process, you must always maintain a correct attitude because your Australian Shepherd puppy will become attached and bond to you even more after receiving some positive vibes.

You need to be loving, kind, patient, and inspiring, showing more happiness and pride than frustration or anger. If you are angry or sad, step away for a few minutes, he will breathe deeply and return to your puppy after calming down.

Only come back if you feel calm, focused, and balanced so that you can continue to train your Australian Shepherd properly. Making him do activities in a negative mood will ruin your dog's mood and leave him with a bad memory of the training experience, with unsatisfactory results for both of you.

Socialization with the puppy transforms it into the type of dog you want when it reaches adulthood. During the first 10 months of life, the dog assumes most of the looks and characteristics for the rest of its life.

Therefore, you have to work right away in this period to reach your final goal; the sooner you do it, the better; this is the standard rule of every workout. Build a plan, stick to it and always be consistent and clear about what you want from your Australian Shepherd puppy.

If he does something you asked him to do, be happy and excited and reward him generously. You will become a great teacher if you stick to these rules and pay attention to your behaviors.

To create a unique and special bond between you and your Australian Shepherd, you must continue with proper socialization, teaching him first that you are the teacher, love him insanely, and want to do everything to become best friends.

Study the advice given in this training guide carefully and always treat your Australian Shepherd puppy as your best friend; in this way, it will become the sweetest creature you have ever had by your side.

Socialize your dog with the right attitude, showing him that you want to be his best friend while making him understand that you are the leader of the pack, you are the dominant friend.

You must be kind and decisive simultaneously; you must give him the necessary information and avoid being aggressive or brutal. You must be firm and motivated when socializing with your Australian Shepherd puppy.

Humans become frustrated and impatient over time and begin neglecting their dogs when they grow up and are no longer cute, calm, and obedient puppies as before.

Many dogs are cruelly left to their fate during the teenage emotional storm. You must never allow yourself to indulge your dog if you feel frustrated or angry with him. In this case, you will have to work harder to educate and pass on all the good he deserves.

With understanding, perseverance, consistency, patience, and the correct information, you can overcome the difficult period of your dog's adolescence and forge an even stronger and lasting bond.

2.6 How important is it to spend time with your Aussie?

You should include time with your Aussie in your daily schedule.

This does not necessarily require an unlimited time, but a few minutes to caress it while watching TV you have to find it every day.

An Australian Shepherd is peaceful and prosperous when he can spend time with his owner.

If you can make time each day to spend with your Aussie, you will find that he is a beautiful friend who will make you happy.

CHAPTER 3: Be prepared for the arrival of your Australian Shepherd puppy

Before your Australian Shepherd puppy arrives in your home, you need to consider the number of supplies you need to purchase. Even if you are excited and can't wait for your puppy to walk through the front door of your home, there are several things you need to worry about.

Your pet shop's list of supplies usually recommended does not have to be fully respected, but what you need to have before your puppy arrives is very simple.

You will learn in this chapter what supplies are needed and optional supplies, as well as how you can turn your home into a real palace for your puppy.

3.1 The supplies your puppy needs

You need to have some things before you bring your puppy home, but you don't need to have a lot of things, so you need to make a selection.

You must arrange the food in the puppy bowls before their arrival to avoid taking them to the supermarket before they have had their scheduled vaccinations.

We will now go into detail on all the supplies your puppy needs.

3.1.1 The collar

The most suitable collar for your Australian Shepherd puppy is the flat one; make sure you have at least one before your arrival. You should buy a cheap nylon collar and not an expensive collar as puppies increase, and the collar may not suit your dog after a short time. The most comfortable collar for your puppy to wear is the one that allows you to insert two fingers between the collar and his throat.

3.1.2 Brushes for grooming

The Australian Shepherd does not typically require a lot of care, but they must be brushed regularly to keep them clean and tidy. Surely you will not need as many tools as the minimum ones required for each type of grooming.

3.1.3 Bowls for water and food

Your Australian Shepherd puppy must always have a bowl of water and food that he can reach easily. The best bowl to buy is stainless steel, as it is easy to clean, does not allow bacteria to grow, is durable, and does not break.

You could also opt for a nice ceramic bowl, as long as it can be washed in the dishwasher; however, it allows bacteria to grow inside the ceramic bowl breaks.

You do not have to buy plastic bowls because your puppy may be allergic to plastic, thus causing a reaction on the muzzle and nose and because the scratches on the plastic could cause bacteria to grow.

3.1.4 The leash

For the size and characteristics of an Australian Shepherd puppy, it is advisable to purchase a leash that is at least two meters long and perhaps matches the collar.

Next, the leash must be comfortable and sturdy to hold in your hand. Next, you will need a leash of at least 20 feet to teach your Australian Shepherd the command "come."

3.1.5 Toys

You don't have to think that toys for puppies and dogs are just one more thing; on the contrary, they are necessary.

For example, if your Australian Shepherd puppy puts something in his mouth and starts chewing it, you can give him a toy to distract him from chewing.

It is much better to buy toys to entertain and delight your puppy than to spend more money repairing your kitchen or living room furniture.

3.1.6 Crate for home training

You should buy a crate for your puppy's home training, even if you may not like the idea of putting one inside the house. This tool will protect your dog when you can't look at him or even stay outside.

The crates are a den for most puppies who enjoy playing with them and spending time inside; they are not a prison for dogs, although some may think so.

In addition, the chests become a safe place to relax and sleep; dogs are living beings, and they need a safe place where they know they can sleep peacefully without running into danger.

3.1.7 The bed for your Aussie

Another necessary supply is the kennel for your Aussie. You could use blankets or a faux sheepskin rug to make the kennel even more comfortable. Even if you usually allow him to get on the sofa at home, your puppy must always have a comfortable place to lie in his crate.

3.1.8 Household cleaning products

Cleaning products for your home are necessary and must be purchased before your Australian Shepherd puppy arrives.

In particular, you need to buy floor and carpet cleaners that contain specific enzymes to get rid of dirt even more thoroughly.

Do not use toxic cleaning products as they could harm your puppy, and he may lick your feet, paws, or even the floor itself. Before buying, you must check that the detergents are natural and do not contain alcohol or solvents.

Also, buy paper handkerchiefs and napkins.

3.2 Making your home suitable for your puppy

You and your Australian Shepherd will begin a beautiful journey together if your home is comfortable and suited to their needs. The Australian Shepherd is like an intelligent and curious little boy; therefore, he could search and investigate anywhere in your home and destroy it.

For this reason, you need to make your home puppy-proof before walking through the front door. You can do this with excellent results if you follow the tips and tricks we will discuss in the following pages.

3.2.1 Observe everything from the puppy's point of view

You must rummage and crawl around the house before your Aussie arrives. You will continue to do this at least twice a week. Look at objects from your puppy's point of view and pick up paperclips, drawing pins, pieces of paper, wood splinters, or anything else dangerous to your puppy.

Collect and tidy up your clothes as they can be a very high source of danger; socks, for example, can suffocate your Australian Shepherd puppy.

3.2.2 Close all access to water

Close the toilet lids, sinks, and drain tanks and completely block access to the pool if it is present in the garden of your home.

The water can attract an Australian Shepherd a lot but remember that any puppy dog can still swim well; falling into the water could cause him to drown.

3.2.3 Remove all dangerous objects

You must collect and hide any objects or tools that can be a source of danger to your Australian Shepherd puppy. These must be removed immediately:

- chemicals for lawns, swimming pools, or plants;

- fluids for vehicles (antifreeze);

- drugs;

- tobacco and similar products;

- vitamins and energy products;

- detergents and household cleaning products;

- salt for the ice.

3.2.4 Arrange electrical cables and curtain cables

Your puppy may be attracted to electrical cords by biting and chewing on them. Arrange electrical wires out of the puppy's reach and tidy up lamp cables hanging from furniture, as the puppy could pull them down while playing.

Hide as much as possible or, in any case, arrange your PC's telephone cables and cables well.

Tidy up and pull up the curtain lines, which could strangle your puppy if he gets tangled around them.

3.2.5 Do not allow your puppy to climb stairs

Your Australian Shepherd puppy must not go upstairs; block the stairs from both above and below.

It could be hazardous for your puppy to climb stairs, as he does not have perfect coordination and may fall. To avoid your puppy tumbling down the stairs and getting hurt, block them before he gets inside.

3.2.6 Put the waste in a particular container

You need to keep litter out of sight of your puppy, perhaps putting it in a particular container.

The garbage can could be an object of your puppy's desire; you must always keep it in a position that your puppy cannot reach, and you must empty it every evening, especially if your puppy does not sleep in his crate but freely around the house.

Also, hide bathroom trash baskets as they are dangerous for your American Shepherd, as they may contain used **cotton balls**, **razor blades**, **Q-tips**, **razors**, **scissors**, etc.

3.2.7 Close all doors

Open doors may intrigue your puppy, so you must always keep them closed, especially if they lead outside your home.

3.2.8 Keep objects and ornaments aloft

Remove all objects and ornaments on tables and shelves and place them as high as possible, and your puppy may reach out and drop them. Always keep them out of his reach; his wagging tail could throw them off balance.

By hiding or placing these items on top, you will also prevent your puppy from putting them in his mouth and risk suffocating.

You don't have to do this forever until your Australian Shepherd understands what he can and cannot touch.

3.3 Making the external environment safe

To make the home safe for your puppy, check the outside carefully. Look for and clear any openings in the fence and objects that can be dangerous to your Australian Shepherd puppy.

For example, drain pipes, swimming pools, or other things in the garden can be hazardous.

Collect all dangerous items and put fences around the pool or drain pipes. You must make the external environment safe at the same level as the internal environment.

3.3.1 The right place for your needs

The outside cannot become the specific place for his needs, and you probably don't want your puppy to consider the whole yard as his toilet, especially if you also have children.

You have to be strategic and take him to the exact spot where you want him to go to the bathroom.

When you stand there, please give him a specific one-word command so that he will quickly learn to go to the right place every time he hears this command.

Choose another simple command to use when you want him to do his business.

This command will help him remember what to do and will be very useful when you are out and about and need to teach him a new place away from home to go to the toilet.

You must choose a word that will not embarrass you in public, such as **"get busy"** or **"mind your own business**."

3.3.2 Check indoor and outdoor plants

You have to check the plants you have inside and outside the house.

If you have poisonous plants for dogs, remove them or place them in areas of the home that your Australian Shepherd puppy cannot reach easily.

Ultimately, to make your home safe for your puppy, you need to keep it clean and tidy and take some precautions.

Whoever lives in your home needs to work with you to keep the space clean and need to check if the house is still puppy safe constantly.

CHAPTER 4: Education and training in the first weeks with your Australian Shepherd puppy

4.1 Everything you need to know about the first days at home

The first thing you need to do when your Australian Shepherd puppy arrives home is to take him outside, where you have decided, he will go to the toilet. He will learn where to go every time his pee or poop escapes.

Create space inside the house for your puppy: take other pets outside or put the children in the room; your new friend needs space and time to acclimate to his new kingdom. Teach family members to remain calm and kind when they see the puppy and only approach him if he wishes and does not fidget.

Australian Shepherd puppies react differently when they enter a new home; some explore the house far and wide, some fall asleep, and others observe the surrounding environment from the sidelines.

Place your puppy immediately in its fenced area after preparing it with the appropriate pads for needs, a bowl with water, a crate with blankets inside, chew toys, and a blanket outside the crate. Getting him used to his territory is a great idea.

The first day in his new home may be less likely than expected. Your puppy may have been transported by car or plane, or maybe it comes directly from a shelter and may be tired and sleepy. Rest assured that the next day will be much more eventful as the puppy will be more rested.

In the first few days or even the first few weeks, your puppy may cry, howl or scream as he may be suffering from separation anxiety. He may also have difficulty falling asleep and staying still; he will gradually get used to being away from his mother, brothers, and sisters who cuddled him up until recently.

Another tip you must follow is to move slowly when introducing your new friend to other pets already in the house. Place a crate with a gate or a fence to create a barrier that allows them to adapt to each other, avoiding direct and risky physical contact.

After a week, have your puppy visit the vet for a general check-up and immediately show concern for his health and physical condition.

4.2 How to prevent bad behaviour from becoming a habit

Like any person, your dog also likes to feel comfortable, safe, and with the family in their own space. To avoid many problems of acclimatization that could arise, you should make the living area adequate.

Try to minimize any noises your puppy will hear from the first days in your home, such as appliance noises and mechanical noises, which can only scare your puppy because he has never heard them before.

You must help your Australian Shepherd puppy by giving him treats and toys and always praising him during the training and socialization phases.

To counter the problems that may arise in the following years, you must always reward his calm behavior and show authority and control towards his favorite things. Remember that dogs are natural and social creatures. Communicating with them is important; communication is the most important element in making their behavior more stable.

You need to keep your Australian Shepherd happy. Give him adequate exercise physical and always keep him mentally active.

You have to let him spend a lot of time with other dogs or people, and you must always pay attention to his diet; you must give him healthy, nutritious, and suitable food for your dog's needs, avoiding excessive portions or fatty foods.

The Australian Shepherd, like all dogs, is a pack animal and therefore needs to be sure that you are its strong and dominant leader. You must never leave your dog with doubts about who is boss between the two, regardless of the situations that may arise.

Your **Australian Shepherd** will have no problems and will feel strong and confident if he is aware that he has a strong leader to follow, thus working on getting him his well-deserved rewards. But, of course, before giving him any prizes or gifts, you must always ensure that he is polite and calm.

You need to understand what motivates your dog's behavior; this is the first step to helping him overcome life's challenges. Certain behaviors such as barking, chewing, jumping, chasing, digging, pulling, or orbiting the leash are common to dogs because of their character and genes. However, these behaviors are different in the dog we train at home.

For example, barking to attract attention or pushing our hands to be caressed are behaviors strengthened by contact with people and are not innate. For this, they should never be rewarded.

You need to understand what motivates your dog or not. Maybe ask yourself why he doesn't come to you when you call him while playing with other dogs. This behavior occurs because he prefers to be with other beings of the same species than with you.

You could change this by giving him a treat, pampering him a little, and then allowing him to go back to playing with his furry friends.

Do this work out slowly and close to where he is playing. When you call your dog, walk away and show yourself distracted; after he starts coming to you regularly, pet him, verbally praise him and give him treats.

4.3 The behavioural problems of separation anxiety

Separation anxiety is when a dog feels depressed and distressed after separating from its owner. This situation almost always arises within an hour of the separation from its owner and represents one of the most challenging problems when you decide to get a dog.

Symptoms deriving from separation anxiety occur in adult dogs but especially in puppies which begin when they move away from their siblings, little sisters, and mother for the first time.

In adult dogs, anxious behaviors vary according to character, although they can almost always be traced back to separation from the original family when they were puppies. Likewise, a traumatic event, such as a physical injury, neglect, or mistreatment, can cause anxiety in a dog; however, these events derive from a brutal and clear separation from his master.

Therefore, we can affirm that the reasons that cause the anxious behaviors, although different, always have the same primary reason.

With the passing of age, some problems caused by dog aging, such as loss or lowering of sight and hearing, could increase or exacerbate anxiety levels, generating unstable behaviors. Therefore, it is essential to learn to understand health behaviors and wrong behaviors, recognize the first signs and symptoms, and take action to minimize the negative consequences.

As soon as it arrives in a new home, the Australian Shepherd puppy may exhibit behaviors that may seem strange to you. The constant desire and request for contact and demonstrations of affection, the continuous moans and crying, and the need to follow your movements clearly show that your puppy suffers from separation anxiety.

However, these behaviors are expected as the puppy is experiencing new sensations in unfamiliar territory for the first time.

The anxiety generated in the puppy will create a survival instinct that will make it remain attached to its owner; for this, you must consider such behavior regular and predictable.

If you leave your puppy alone for a long time in the first few days, he will bark, cry and strongly express his discomfort at the lonely state he is feeling. During your absence, the duration of these behaviors will be determined by the character and personality your dog can develop.

When he is alone, your puppy will start moaning and whimpering and calm down after about half an hour by chewing or gnawing on one of his rubber toys. These behaviors are expected during the first days and nights but will not last indefinitely.

You must have the patience to put up with its annoying sounds and complaints only in the first period; after a few weeks, your puppy will adapt to his new home and develop the character accompanying him for the rest of his life.

You must remember that the behaviors he exhibits in the first period may seem upsetting, but in reality, they are normal and will subside over time.

Healthy training and consistent socialization will allow your Australian Shepherd puppy to overcome these anxieties and gain self-confidence, becoming an adult dog well integrated into his life context. Mental and physical training is essential for strengthening a puppy's character, but they are not enough to completely cure separation anxiety.

4.3.1 Ways to prevent separation anxiety

Here are some methods to prevent separation anxiety and all the potential behavioral problems.

- Your Australian Shepherd puppy is cuddly and probably one of the sweetest things you've come across. As soon as you saw him in the litter, you immediately fell in love with him, so you took him and brought him home to become a new family member. Although the desire to pet, cuddle, pet, and hold your puppy is immense and probably inherent in human nature, in these moments, you need to be moderate and aloof to ensure his good.

- Leave the puppy alone often from the moment you bring him home. First, keep it out of your sight, then put it in its crate or inside its gated space. These first periods of separation must have short durations, at most 5 minutes each; when you see your puppy going through these intervals in solitude without fidgeting or complaining excessively, it increases without exaggerating the time he is left alone. Do this at least three or four times a day; during this period, it is essential to ignore any complaints or manifestations of anxiety and not confuse this attitude with negligence or superficiality.

- You must give your puppy a space of his own, whether he stays awake or falls asleep. Distance and autonomy create healthy independence since it is neither negligence nor malice. This distance is essential for him to develop proactive measures to help him feel confident when alone.

4.3.2 How to build a healthy relationship with your Australian Shepherd puppy

Always check your reactions and temperament when your puppy screams to get your attention.

You must stay composed and calm when your Aussie gets angry and complains, even if he makes your head pop with his crying, howling, and barking. Remember that you always command and dictate rules and schedules, not your furry friend; therefore, remain firm and balanced in your actions and behaviors.

4.4 The naming of your puppy

You can start teaching your Australian Shepherd puppy the commands and tricks after correctly responding to the click sound and recognizing that the follow this sound.

You must teach your puppy some essential things, including the basic exercise through which he responds to his name.

Indeed, you've gone through the lengthy process of naming your puppy by now, and it's only fitting that now whenever his word is spoken, your Aussie knows how to respond. This is fun, satisfying, and not too difficult if you do it right.

This training to teach your puppy his name is necessary always to get and keep his attention when you call him.

Make sure you have a wide variety of treats and tasty foods before training. Take these treats and put them in your pocket, bag, or home furniture out of sight and reach of your puppy.

1) Don't pay attention to your puppy until he looks directly at you; ignore him completely. Then, when he looks at you, click and give him a treat; repeat this action

20 times, so you can teach your puppy to associate the click with a tasty tidbit when he looks at you.

2) When the puppy observes it carefully, shout its name aloud before clicking and giving it the treat.

3) Do this repeatedly until your Australian Shepherd puppy turns around and looks at you when you say his name.

4) Gradually reduce your Aussie's click and pleasure each time he looks at you. You have to increase this decrease: first, once out of two, then, once in three, out of four until you get to do nothing. **You don't have to get rid of the C / T too quickly.**

Also, after recognizing his name, a **click-delirium** (C/T) should be performed from time to time to keep the puppy's memory fresh and reinforce the idea and association between hearing his name and receiving a treat.

Finally, you must observe your Australian Shepherd puppy's attitude, skills, and rhythm during this period and adjust accordingly when needed. The Aussie's goal is to obey your commands through physical or vocal signals without demanding any reward.

The most important behavior to learn is knowing how to respond to your name because it is the fundamental skill that will serve him throughout his future training.

Therefore, you will have to devote time and a lot of attention to this training until it is appropriately completed, and you can continue with the subsequent phases.

CHAPTER 5: Learning the basic commands

5.1 What are the basic commands of the dog

On the following pages, you will find many basic commands you will need to teach your dog. First, you must choose a quiet and isolated place to work with your puppy for about 25 minutes for each command.

Training must be done from the first days and can be more effective if you use the leash for greater control; later, you could switch to off-leash training when you observe that it begins to follow basic commands safely.

COME

A well-behaved dog comes when called. You can start teaching them this command by telling your Australian Shepherd puppy to come to you and rewarding him with a tasty treat.

You must only give him the prize after he comes to you. At this point, he begins to say "Come" in different tones and especially when he is busy playing or is intrigued by a game; you have to reward him only if he comes to you and, if he ignores you, repeat the command until the moment he comes to you.

He gradually eliminates the gifts and prizes and will go to you whenever he is called, no matter what happens.

SIT

One of the first commands to teach your Australian Shepherd puppy is to "sit." If he can sit down by himself, tell him, "Have a good session," click and reward him. He then starts training him well to make him sit up for you, and when his paw touches the floor, you click and reward him. You could also show him the specific movement by pushing his butt to the floor, but he remembers to click and reward him when he sits down.

DOWN

The moment your Australian Shepherd naturally lies down, click and reward him by saying, "Good," whenever you see him lying down, give the command "Down." You must teach him the command before using it in the training phase.

When you are sure, he has learned and understood what "Down" means, he starts using this command and makes him lie down; click and reward him if he lies down at your command.

Take it out and try this type of workout in various places. First, you must teach him that no matter where he lies down, he can only receive a click and a reward if he obeys your command.

Then, slowly eliminate the treats and clicks if you see that he is comfortable when he lies down on your command.

STAY

Teach your puppy to stay still in one seat by making him sit down. After he sits down, wait a few seconds, click and reward him. You must do this many times, increasing the time your dog sits and waits.

Finally, give him the command "Stay," keeping a flat palm on his face when you are and, after a few seconds, click and reward him if he stays still. If, on the other hand, he moves and comes towards you, he starts all over again without rewarding him; the rule for receiving the prize is that he must sit still.

When you see your Aussie improve their training by staying still for more than a minute at a time, you can move on to the next level. He backs up and says, "Stay": obviously, he will want to get up suddenly and come to you, but you have to bring him back in his place by repeating the command "Stay," making the signal with your hand.

Go away again and only reward your puppy when he can stay still for as long as possible. Raise the level of training by increasing it by two minutes at a time between the session and the prize.

You can also train by giving him the command to stay and leave the room or otherwise go out of sight. When he remains, reward him with praise or a gift, but if he doesn't stay still, repeat the exercise until your puppy does it correctly.

FETCH

Get a toy your dog loves and start playing with him. When you throw the toy, tell him the word "Fetch," click and give him the prize only when he takes the object and brings it back to you. Your puppy will learn to get any item back to you every time you say "Fetch" because he knows you will reward him.

To teach them this type of command in any situation, you need to point to an item and shout "Fetch," click and reward it. Over time, as your Australian Shepherd becomes faster and more skilled in retrieving the object you throw at him, he eliminates the reward.

DROP IT

If your Australian Shepherd puppy puts something in his mouth he shouldn't, you can use the command to drop it as soon as you tell him. Give him a toy he likes and while he plays with it, bring candy or treat to his nose and say the phrase "Drop it." At this point, he will drop the toy to get the reward, and you will have to click and reward it.

After doing some training, he starts hiding the treats. Try this command at least 10-15 times a day until he drops what's in his mouth for a joy he can't see; you will see that by continuing with this type of training, you will be able to eliminate the delicacies and he will still drop what he has in his mouth when you command it.

LEAVE IT

This command will help you not let your Australian Shepherd puppy eat or touch things you don't want. Through this exercise, you can distract him from seeing a lizard or rabbit, make him stop chewing on something, or convince him not to touch the waste during your walks.

You must take two morsels in both hands, making him smell one. Then he starts not to show you interest to make him understand that he will not receive any prize, click and give him the tip using the other hand.

Open your hand, show him the treat and close it as soon as he tries to take it. Repeat this exercise until he ignores the hand because he knows he won't get the reward.

When he ignores it, click and reward him with the other hand; you might even say the word "Leave it" if he pays attention to this hand to encourage him to learn the command more easily.

Go to the next level of training by placing the treat on the floor with your open hand. You will see that he will run to get it, and you will have to cover him with your hand and shout, "Leave it."

When he ignores that hand covering the tidbit, click and give him the treat; then, show him the prize and stand up saying "Leave it," and if he does, reward him with pleasure using the other hand.

Train him in a variety of settings and situations. For example, train him while playing in the backyard or neighborhood park, walk him by letting him leave the toys he plays with, or drop the treats he has in his mouth.

CHAPTER 6: The Perfect Discipline to Avoid Your Aussie's Misbehaviour

6.1 Do not make him chew on harmful or inappropriate things

Your Australian Shepherd, even when it becomes an adult, chews your fingers, house rugs, shoes, table legs, and any other furniture or object other than a dog toy. If this happens, you must not get angry with him, but you must first train and monitor your dog's movements, distracting him and making him do other things.

You need to understand why your Aussie is chewing because teething is painful for the puppy, and chewing relieves the pain caused by growing adult teeth.

To allow your puppy to chew and, therefore, to relieve the pain of teething, make sure he has plenty of chew toys and a thick, ice-cold, knotted, water-soaked towel to chew on at all times.

By the time your Aussie gets older, has outgrown adult teeth, and continues to chew on your kitchen table legs just like toys, you probably haven't been paying attention. You haven't taken the time to secure your dog's daily exercises he needs.

Also, you haven't taught your puppy what can be chewed and what shouldn't be chewed with a firm and convincing "**NO**"; you should have replaced the table legs with a chewable toy, praising and rewarding him when he could do that.

6.2 Excessive excitement and agitation from visits

You must keep your Australian Shepherd from getting overly excited when your friends visit you. As soon as your Aussie walks through the front door, teach him to be calm and not aroused, especially when he sees others.

An excited and agitated dog should always be ignored and only be touched when calm and relaxed; otherwise, you will inadvertently make him realize that it is normal and acceptable to be aroused when he sees a human being.

If your friends or relatives come to visit you at home, and your Australian Shepherd is overly aroused, you need to stand in between them, creating a precise space in which you have to yell at your dog the word **"Go"** and ask your friends or your relatives not to consider it.

Your puppy, if properly trained, will have learned to sit on command to be more easily controlled.

6.3 Do not let him pull on the leash

You must spend time teaching your dog to pad on your leash and have him put on the training collar right away to prevent him from pulling on the leash.

Buy a sturdy training collar and adjust it properly; as soon as your puppy tries to pull forward, give the collar a sharp tug towards yourself and shout the word **"Heel"** vehemently.

Until your dog understands what he needs to do, repeat this movement for a few minutes a day for several days. Remember that every dog has his character and is different, so you must insist with conviction until he learns well.

He can help you go round in circles or do eight and suddenly change direction while he is on a leash. This movement will teach your dog a correct walking position while preventing it from being trampled.

6.4 Prevent him from stealing food or rummaging through the trash

The Australian Shepherd is a dog that likes food very much, and being athletic, it will be easy for him to jump from one part of the room to the other or on the false ceilings.

Therefore, you must not give him the opportunity for tempting food, as he will steal it without you even noticing.

To ensure this and avoid any theft by your Aussie, you must be vigilant and never leave food unattended in places that can be reached with ease.

6.5 Aggressive walking

You need to ensure that your dog does not act aggressively during a walk but walks calmly without pulling on the leash.

When you walk next to your dog, you must make him understand that you are his master and leader, responsible for every situation, preventing him from protecting you at any cost from any position or external stimulus.

Firmly tug on his collar shouting "**NO!**" if he does such a thing; you must constantly remind him who is in charge.

6.6 Jumping constantly to get your attention

The puppy might always jump because he expects constant attention from you. You are the world to your dog, and very often, when he is still and silent in a place of the house, you forget him.

Also, when you walk together, you may think about other things like your car, your wife, work, dinner, holidays, or ignoring your faithful companion who respectfully walks beside you. Your dog only gets your attention when he jumps on you for these reasons.

At this point, you look at him, are amazed, and scold him by pushing him down until he lies down on the ground. You keep ignoring him and promise to teach him not to jump on you again in the future. But you didn't understand anything! Your dog wants your attention.

You must patiently teach him that your attention will only come if he is planted on the ground with all four legs and not if he jumps on you.

Do not punish your Aussie while training him not to jump on people.

Don't shout words like **"Bad!"** or **"No!"** and **don't push him to his knees on the ground**.

Instead, you must turn around and ignore him to manage his continuous jumps.

6.7 Digging

Even if you do everything to prevent this, some dogs will dig. Some dogs are born diggers, and this behavior is innate and natural for them, having to act in this way by necessity. You won't be able to avoid these behaviors easily, whether they depend on foraging or hunting, because they are ingrained in their DNA. When your dog is a digger, to prevent him from escaping from the garden of your home, you will have to fence your guard very profoundly and thus keep them safe inside your garden or yard.

Some dogs have the instinctive urge to dig for more food; this could be the reason why your dog digs hard and vehemently into your garden.

Dogs are omnivores, so they could uproot bulbs, rhizomes, tubers, or any edible vegetable hidden in the ground. They may be attracted to newly sprouted herbs, squirrel-buried nuts, rotting carcasses, or other strong smells that will prompt their sensitive noses to dig deeper and deeper.

Sometimes dogs may also dig out of boredom, lack of physical exercise, mental training, or poor socialization. Dogs that have socialized improperly could suffer from separation anxiety or other behavioral problems, while uncastrated dogs could dig an escape route to reach a female in heat.

A working breed like the Australian Shepherd could create the problem of constant digging if it is not kept busy with physical and mental exercises.

The smell of specific soil types could attract a dog's imagination: damp earth, some mulch, fresh earth, and sand are possible baits for the digging dog. If your dog has this trait, you should fence off the areas where you use these soil types.

You must also pay attention to freshly potted plants, flower beds, and flowers in your garden.

Physical and mental exercise and proper socialization will help you fight your burrowing dog. Remember that some digging dogs will always be able to dig regardless of the situation and place they are found.

6.8 Excessive barking

A dog barks for various reasons, but it barks to get the owner's attention most of the time. Your Aussie may be barking because he is close to mealtime and wants food, fun, or attention.

A dog can also bark to warn that there are intruders, so it is essential to understand why our dog barks. Not all barking is terrible: some can be short-lived, others can go on for hours and hours, and we want to get it to stop as soon as possible, preventing things from getting out of control.

Either way, you shouldn't pay attention to the barking dog and shouldn't send out signals that assume you are reacting immediately, such as seeing why it is barking or how to move towards it.

If the cause is misbehavior that needs to be corrected, shout "Forget it" and ignore it. As you do this, move from one side of the room to the other or even leave the room, and you can also close the door behind you until your dog has calmed down.

You must clarify to your dog that barking is not for reward or attention.

In everyday life, make sure you do activities that the dog likes but you always decide. You must always show your Australian Shepherd puppy that you are the undisputed leader and in charge.

You must make him understand what you give him as a reward if he is to earn it and that he must be calm and seated to receive a prize.

6.9 Nipping

Little Australian Shepherd puppies are friendly and aggressive and may bite for various reasons, including getting your attention. If you own a wire cutter, don't worry too much, as your puppy will stop having this behavior over time.

The Australian Shepherd bites by instinct because it is bred for herding and needs to demonstrate its strength toward family members, such as other pets or children.

Do not punish or correct your puppy while he is in the biting phase, as it could lead to problems in the future.

You must, however, make your Australian Shepherd puppy understand how delicate men's skin is by getting him to bite and give him feedback.

When he bites, express your disapproval to him with words such as "**Youch!**" or "**Yipe!**" or show him the physical pain you feel by returning with the body part he bit. In this way, your puppy will understand that this is not the right behavior.

Once this is done, you need to start ignoring the dog, as it serves to make him understand that excessive attention reinforces negative behavior.

If you show yourself sensitive to his bites, your puppy will know that humans are susceptible and that they respond to physical pain with concrete and sudden vocal manifestations.

CHAPTER 7: Your Australian Shepherd's Training Disciplines

7.1 Click training

Training your dog with the clicker is a helpful way to get inside his head and prompt his subconscious to act instinctively on command after a specific command has been taught.

Clicker training uses a device that emits a noise (**"click"**) that teaches your Australian Shepherd to associate the sound with a direct command and a reward following that command. Dogs, in general, are rapidly learning through conditioning, and the clicker is useful for strengthening this conditioning.

The clicker is an educational device, and you must understand immediately that you won't always use it. After your Australian Shepherd has learned to follow your commands, you can take the clicker off and no longer need it. Likewise, you won't have to carry it throughout your dog's life unless you like to hear the sound of a click, regardless of its use.

The treats are not the only rewards you can offer, although they are very effective during your Australian Shepherd puppy training. In addition to giving these rewards, you could give your puppy a toy or other occasional gift to reward his calm and commendable demeanor.

Show him and hide it so he will have to guess and eagerly await his reward as a reward for his obedience.

The treats you give your puppy don't have to be loaded with calories and sugar. The best things to give your dog are small treats, such as a grain of corn or a piece of dried meat, which you can find in countless varieties at any supermarket. If you give your puppy small treats, he won't get tired, won't get lazy, and won't get fat, even though you decide to reward him often. You can quickly put them in your pocket using a dog snack case purchased online or at any pet store in your city. But permanently hide these tidbits.

For example, when you are trying to teach your dog to sit, give him the command to sit, and only after he obeys do you reward him with a treat.

In your dog's training session, the clicker works as a modeler and must be used with progressive and gradual steps to teach the desired command. You have to reward him every time he executes an order and an action you want.

You will also need to add more time to keep the command in each subsequent phase, and eventually, your Aussie will be able to associate the click noise with a reward. He will have to understand that a reward will be given if he hears the clicking sound.

The conditioning will become so strong that he will no longer need the clicker and the tidbit at some point, but he will only do what you command.

Why is the clicker more effective than the word "good" or of any other word?

The clicker is a unique and unmistakable sound that your dog cannot mistake for any other sound or signal. The human voice can change pitch and sound in different situations, while some commands always sound the same in many words we use. On the other hand, the click never varies in terms of sound and volume and is coherent and reassuring.

7.2 Leash training

Training on a leash is one of the most complicated exercises you will have to teach your Australian Shepherd puppy. This practice takes a lot of time and work, but it is gratifying by strengthening the bond and trust between you and your Australian Shepherd puppy if done correctly.

The leash is the rope that binds you to your faithful companion and must be sturdy, adjustable, of good quality, and with a resistant collar and harness. You can choose from many collars, and you should search among the different types available on the market to buy the best one for your Aussie.

Possible choices are collars and front attachment harnesses; you need to be sure they fit well, are the correct size, and your dog feels comfortable wearing them.

When buying a collar, you need to consider some essential aspects. If your dog is large, but you are small, or if your dog is powerful and aggressive, you will have to put in a lot of effort to control him, so you should get a sturdy collar.

Collars with front attachment are recommended for any dog and any activity and should be used with leashes 6 feet (1.84 meters) or less in length. The leash needs to be shorter to prevent your dog from picking up speed enough to injure himself when the leash ends, suddenly becoming stiff.

Leash training mainly aims to let your dog walk next to you without pulling the leash. One way to do this exercise well would be to stop walking forward when your dog pulls on the leash, turn around, continue walking in the opposite direction, and reward him with praise and treats if he obediently walks beside you.

This way, you will be able to reinforce the desired behavior and train your Australian Shepherd puppy to have good manners on a leash. Always remember that the ultimate goal is to walk without a leash.

Before completing this training, you must ensure that your Australian Shepherd puppy correctly performs the specific action of the training phase it is carrying out. His consistency and work are necessary to succeed in this training, so don't rush but take all the time your dog needs.

7.3 Train your puppy to be obedient

You need to train your Australian Shepherd puppy to be obedient. Obedience will allow the puppy to live with positive interactions and create a stronger bond with you and with other humans.

It is essential to teach your simple puppy commands like **"come,"** **"down,"** **"stop,"** and **"sit"** that will help keep your Aussie dog safe and in control in any situation that could be dangerous. One idea might be to take an obedience training course to allow you and your dog to learn the best ways for each situation and command.

If your puppy learns to be obedient, he will be able to interact with other people and dogs of all ages and origins. Positive reinforcement is a much more effective and satisfying process than punishment.

7.4 Bath training

If you wish to keep your home clean, you need to do some home training exercises; before that, you should find a suitable place for your Australian Shepherd puppy to go to the bathroom.

Since your puppy has not yet received all the required vaccinations as soon as he arrives home, you will need to find a bathroom not accessible to other animals to prevent your little friend from catching a virus or other diseases.

When training your puppy to be housebroken, the three basic things to consider are positive reinforcement, planning, and patience.

Laud your puppy when it goes to the bathroom outside, and don't punish him when unexpected events occur that could not otherwise be avoided.

The following times are recommended for trying to give your Australian Shepherd puppy a proper bathing routine.

- before your puppy goes to sleep;

- when you wake up;

- after your puppy has eaten or drank water;

- when the puppy wakes up;

- before and after physical exercise.

CHAPTER 8: Learning to understand your Australian Shepherd's language

8.1 Tones, movements, and body language

Understanding your Aussie's movements and body tones may seem very difficult, but it is unique and exciting.

You have to be good at building a healthy and lasting relationship with your new friend because you are in charge of your relationship; you have to act with the mentality of the pack leader, showing patience, affection, and good.

It is enjoyable to have a faithful and obedient friend always next to you, no matter how things go. The relationship with your Australian Shepherd must be built over time, and after you have started training, you will continue for the whole life of your sweet friend.

If you breed an obedient dog, it will be much easier to care for, and it will cause you fewer problems as well as fewer household expenses.

To understand your dog's messages and be clear about what he is trying to tell you, you must learn to read his gestures, expressions, and body tones.

On the following pages, we will cover dog speech and body language to provide you with all the information your puppy is struggling to convey to you. For you, all of this could prove to be a considerable advantage when training your Aussie.

It is not easy to read a dog's body language correctly, as each of them has their specific personality and will express themselves in their way. One dog might wag his tail because he is happy as another dog because he is nervous or agitated; it is very difficult to interpret a dog's body language.

8.2 The muzzle

Your dog expresses the feelings he is experiencing through pronounced expressions of the muzzle.

Your Australian Shepherd smiles when he pulls his lips back and shows his teeth. With this sunny expression, he wants you to understand that he is happy and calm or feeling excited about something.

If, on the other hand, with a low growl, he shows his fangs and raises his upper lip, it means that he wants to growl at you because you are harming him; in this case, you have to pay close attention, and you have to engage with a quick reaction to make him stop growling.

Even though he is convinced that you will take his food from him, he cannot bark at you and you can do whatever you want without him being able to object.

You may see some dogs getting sad all the time, but that doesn't mean they are; maybe they want to be left alone and relaxed.

When your Australian Shepherd pouts you and looks at you with heartbreaking eyes, he is moaning; not for this, you will have to give in to his gaze and start spoiling him.

8.3 The tail

According to most people, a dog's wagging tail can mean that the dog is happy, curious, scared, confused, confident, or preparing for a fight. In breeds with a small tail, it will be necessary to observe to identify what the tail's position might mean; in this case, it is advisable to rely mainly on the movements and postures of the face and body. Dogs with a docked tail and a flat, black muzzle make it more challenging to understand what they are trying to express.

If you stay away, you may have difficulty understanding the **black-colored dogs'** facial expressions. In breeds with long, puffy fur, it is even more challenging to understand the nature of their gestures and movements.

8.4 Whimpering

Whimpering is always an expression of fear; a dog usually whines when threatened or frightened. He may complain to get your attention when you don't give it to him, get something, or get your help.

8.5 Growling

When your Aussie growls, it means that he wants to be aggressive; growling is a clear sign of aggression. Your puppy will never growl at you but only at strangers when he needs to protect his family, food, and territory.

8.6 Barking

The reasons why dogs can bark are innumerable. Dogs commonly have as a sign of greeting or to attract the owner's attention, they bark at other animals and strangers, or they can bark when they are bored; to avoid this unpleasant situation, you could use a quality collar or train with a clicker.

If he makes short barks while jumping, it means he is feeling aroused and is seeking attention.

8.7 Howling

Would it scare you to imagine the dark silhouette of a dog howling while the full moon is in the background? Consider that a dog's howl has different tones in each breed.

If your Australian Shepherd howls, he is expressing excitement, warning, longing, or loneliness; a single, lonely cry means your pup is looking for an answer, probably from you. Dogs may howl even after a long hunt if they have recognized and encircled their prey.

CHAPTER 9: Hand Signals for Training Your Australian Shepherd

9.1 Usefulness of hand signals

It will benefit you to learn the hand commands to train your Australian Shepherd, in addition to your verbal commands or solely.

Consider the situation where you are making a work call from home and need to seat your Aussie; wouldn't it be better to give him a signal with your hand to let him know to sit down instead of yelling at him, **"Sit down"?** Not verbalizing the command can be useful in many similar situations.

9.2 "Sit" hand signal

To get your dog to sit, you must hold your hand with your palm facing him, making a motion similar to performing the stop.

You can start training it by having the dog sit down and reward it with a click and a small gift. Then try to tell him "**Sit**" by clicking, using the cue of the hand, and giving him a treat.

Practice this way at least twenty times, after which you will be ready to use the cue without a verbal command. Until he sits down, please raise your hand, click and reward him.

You may need to reinforce the concept with your hands. Train like this at least twenty more times. At this point, change the context and train in different places, such as the public park or the backyard.

9.3 "Stay" hand signal

For humans, raising your fist may mean power, but for your puppy, "stand." As soon as he sees this gesture, he will stop moving and remain stationary exactly where he is. So, you have to fold your fingers into a fist and stay with the palm of your hand towards your puppy.

Train initially by giving your dog the verbal command "**Stay**," reward him with a click and a small treat; then, tell him "**Stay**" again while using the cue for his hand and click and reward him only if he stays in place.

Practice this movement at least twenty times, adding a few more seconds every time. Once this is done, you can try to use the cue directly without any verbal commands.

Keep your fist raised until you see that it sits up and stays in its place, hold it for a few moments, click and reward it; practice at least twenty times with this manual splint and gradually begin to increase the residence time until it can stay in position for a full minute. If he does this without any verbal commands, reward him. Then begin to change the context, perhaps by training in different places such as the public park or the backyard.

9.4 "Down" hand signal

With a downward hand signal, you move downward and outward from a flat position. Lower your fingers and arm to a semi-closed position keeping your hand outwards, with your natural crease, while the palm of your hand is directed towards the floor. If your puppy will lie down after seeing it, it means your signal was successful.

With a verbal command, make your puppy lie down, thus starting training. Click and reward him with a treat and then try again by saying **"Down"** with the stick of your hand; click again and give him another reward.

Do this workout at least twenty times. If you feel ready, try using the hand splint without a verbal command, hold your hand down until your puppy sits up, click, and then reward him with a treat.

Have him lie down using his hands to make him more confident about his actions. Train in this way twenty times and start practicing in different places, such as the public park, or the backyard. If your puppy obeys your hand signal without needing a verbal command, reward him with a treat.

9.5 "Leave it" hand signal

If you point your hand down with your index finger raised, you are ordering your dog to mind him or drop something he has taken on the ground. You will use this command to make him stop immediately if he messes with food, annoys another animal, digs a hole, or gets on your shoes.

You have to give him the "**Leave him**" signal right away when he messes up that he shouldn't. If he drops what he took, click and reward him with a small treat.

Give him a bone or a toy that he likes to play with, shout "**Leave him**" with the cue of your hand and, if he obeys, click and reward him. Practice this exercise at least twenty times and when you are ready to use the hand cue without a verbal command, point your hand until it releases what it took; click and reward with a treat.

Force him to leave him with your hands to make him better understand what you want from him. Practice at least twenty times and change where you practice, going to a crowded place. If he obeys without the need for a verbal command, give him a treat.

9.6 "Quiet" hand signal

An effective way to tell your Australian Shepherd to shut up when he brays or barks is to make the "**Ok**" signal with his hand cue. As soon as he sees this sign, he will immediately understand that he must be silent.

You can start training by using a verbal command to get your puppy to calm down; then, click and reward him with a small gift. At this point, say "**Shut up**" using the cue, click and continue exercising. You must do this exercise at least twenty times.

You could try to use the hand cue without a verbal command, keeping the "**Ok**" signal until he stops barking: click and reward him with a reward. Execute this exercise at least 20 times.

Change the context in which you train, perhaps going to the public park or backyard. Always reward him when he obeys your hand signal without needing a verbal command.

Change the context and start practicing in different places, like the courtyard and the audience. Always reward when it does what you want and responds to your hand signal without needing a verbal command.

9.7 "Come" hand signal

The "**Come**" signal can be done by holding the hand with the fingers bent and the palm facing up. You must move your fingers in a forward and backward motion so your puppy understands that he has to get closer to you.

Use a verbal command by asking your Australian Shepherd to come towards you; click and give it a prize. Next, say "**Come**" using the hand cue and click. Practice this exercise at least twenty times, and when you are ready to use the line without verbal command, call him with your hand in this position until he comes; if he obeys, click and give him a small reward.

Again, practice at least twenty times and change your context, going to different places like the public park or the backyard. Reward him only if he does what you want and obeys the hand signal without needing a verbal command.

9.8 "Good Boy" hand signal

With your thumb up and making the "**good boy**" signal, let your Australian Shepherd know he is doing what you want.

If you press your puppy with this signal, you encourage him to continue the desired behavior and make him gain self-confidence.

Begin this training by constantly showing your puppy this signal with your hand when he is behaving well or obeying your command and giving him verbal praise.

Then, after a bit of practice, use the power without verbal praise, click and give him a treat if he behaves the way you want. He will soon understand that the thumbs-up is associated with the fact that he has done well and can therefore receive a reward.

CHAPTER 10: How to Be a Perfect Master for Your Australian Shepherd

10.1 Taking care of your Aussie

A preliminary consideration to be made concerns the living conditions of the Australian Shepherd. For this breed, it is advisable to have a large yard or an outdoor garden as they are very active dogs and are known for their work. If you have an adult Australian Shepherd or once your puppy has grown up, you will need to change how you care for them.

One of the most important things you need to learn is how to take care of your Australian Shepherd since he is just a puppy. Knowing how to care appropriately, feed, and train your Aussie will limit future health problems that he may have and will be essential for every phase and aspect of his existence.

Initially, take him to the vet at least once a month for the first five months; subsequently, it will be enough once each step to become an adult.

When it is an adult dog, you will have to bring it twice a year, and you will have to be careful because it will most likely not resist during the visit.

Getting him to train physically and mentally will ultimately reduce diseases and problems, making him always happy.

10.2 The importance of proper nutrition

The well-being of your Australian Shepherd depends very much on canine nutrition. Of course, his needs and eating habits will change based on age, race, and amount of activity, but you must always ensure suitable food and his physical well-being.

Your Aussie needs to eat four times a day when he's a puppy. You must establish a balanced and consistent eating program, avoiding making him eat too close to the time he goes to sleep.

Then, if he doesn't have the urge to escape in the middle of the night while he's trying to fall asleep, you won't have to wake up and maybe trip over some toys to clean his pee or poop.

The daily portions must be divided into quarters and given to him at specific times during the day. A particular feeding program, nutritional absorption, digestion, and regulation of its metabolism will undoubtedly be better.

Feed your Australian Shepherd only puppy food containing the nutrients needed to grow into a healthy adult dog. To make the food softer and therefore easier to eat and digest, you may want to soak it in hot water.

When your Australian Shepherd becomes an adult and starts eating adult dog food, you may want to reduce feeding to twice a day.

You must continue to feed him by checking his weight and always feeding him at regular and established times; your dog's mental well-being and sense of relaxation depend above all on a correct daily food routine.

Feed him once in the morning and once in the evening according to your schedule. You can also put your foot in the same bowl for both morning and evening.

10.2.1 Which dog food to choose?

Many types of canine food include organic, hypoallergenic, vegetarian, vegan, and natural. You must always choose the best food for your Australian Shepherd so he can reach his full physical and mental potential.

10.2.2 Amount of food to give to your Australian Shepherd

There is no exact method of knowing how much food a dog should eat. Some factors should be considered, such as the number of meals, the type of food, the dog's weight, its metabolic rate, and the amount of exercise performed.

You can directly consult the feeding guide found on any dog food box. The feeding guide recommends food based on the dog's weight, but it may not be correct as the dog may gain weight quickly or even have difficulty gaining weight.

You should speak to your veterinarian about how much food to feed your Australian Shepherd.

10.3 Physical activity is essential for your Australian Shepherd

The health of your beautiful Australian Shepherd depends above all on the physical exercise he can carry out. Like any human being, dogs must continuously exercise to enjoy excellent health.

If your dog does not move, as the years go by, he may be prone to muscle problems, obesity, heart problems, diabetes, or he may get bored, which means he will become an unruly dog.

To avoid this, you must keep your Aussie busy with lots of outdoor games and physical and mental exercise.

You need to set aside at least two hours of physical activity a day for your Australian Shepherd, as he is in dire need of it.

For part of this time, you can get him to do activities by letting him run around in your garden or yard, but for the rest of the time, you have to play with him, perhaps with a ball or a Frisbee. Take him with you on hikes or walks so that you too can exercise.

10.4 Grooming your puppy

Your Australian Shepherd puppy's coat should be brushed at least five times weekly. When your dog is shedding his coat, it would be ideal to touch him daily; since Australian Shepherds have stiff and tangle-prone coats, they should be brushed every day to avoid finding their fur and hair in all corners and on all furniture and clothes.

While you may often be tempted to bathe your Australian Shepherd, you must remember that his skin and hair are kept healthy thanks to his natural oils. However, these oils could be removed by too many washes, so it is advisable to bathe them only once a month.

Another important thing is to ensure that your Australian Shepherd's nails remain short to prevent them from hurting you through scratches.

Your Australian Shepherd uses his fingernails for digging, grabbing, and scratching, so be careful not to leave nails and bits of iron on the floor. If his nails get too stiff, you could have your groomer or vet trim them if he doesn't charge you an exaggerated rate.

You could also cut them yourself if your dog cooperates and if you have a dog-specific nail clipper at home.

Try to get him to brush his teeth at least five times a week to avoid dental problems or gum disease. Purchase a dog toothbrush and toothpaste with meat or the chicken flavor to make the job easier.

Also, check your puppy's eyes daily to ensure they are not swollen, sore, or bleeding. Each time you brush your cat with a cotton ball dipped in warm water, clean out any debris and boogers that may be bothering your eyes.

10.5 How to deal with the most common health problems

Each dog could suffer from different health problems, and each breed has a specific set of common health problems that must be addressed. What you can do is learn the most common health problems of your puppy's breed by observing and analyzing symptoms and signs.

You also need to bring your Australian Shepherd regularly for checkups and visits. Especially in the beginning, your puppy may not want to go to a vet visit, but you could make him overcome this fear by taking him to play in the park both before and after the visit to the vet's office.

With this trick, he will be able to associate a cheerful, carefree, and fun experience with a visit to the vet; if he is good and cooperates during the visit, reward him with a treat when you go to the vet.

Stay close to him during the visit as it will help calm his nerves as he receives the vet's shots.

CHAPTER 11: The characteristics of Alpha dogs

11.1 What does Alpha mean?

The Alpha dog is the charismatic leader within a group of dogs; they will do whatever he asks and respect him for the rest of their existence.

The Alpha dog is usually male, with the consequence that if you have a female dog, it will be easier for you to subdue it. Even if you have a male dog, you will be able to stop it without too many problems as the dog as a species is bred to live with humans and to be submissive in harmony and tranquility.

Your Australian Shepherd is looking for safe guidance to get him right. This means that no dog, even the most aggressive, is not bad but lacks direction. If a dog does not have a guide, he is wild and may behave impetuously.

You must become the Alpha, the leader your dog needs, to give him the commands and keep his behavior under control daily. You will train him, and he will listen to you, becoming a good and polite dog thanks to your guide.

In addition, your puppy needs a single leader to avoid getting confused. Any family member can command and dominate your dog, but only one person can be the alpha leader who makes the final decisions.

Alpha dogs have self-control, intelligence, courage, poise, and confidence and are very affectionate, making them ideal pets. To command, the alpha dog must be not only strong, large, and wild but also wise, intelligent, and charismatic.

These traits and keen mental strength will help the alpha dog play its role as a dominator over the rest of the pack.

Dogs are still the only remaining species that humans dominate. Yet, dogs live happily with humans and are regarded as the best friends a man or woman can have ever since birth. They take their orders from us humans, and they will learn everything we teach them.

Shopping for an adult dog may challenge you as some breeds are more competitive than others. In every family, a member dominates the house dog the most, and he will be the alpha leader.

The undisciplined, untrained, hyperactive dogs that destroy everything they see behave this way because the owner has not succeeded in them, an alpha that is the pack's leader. Unfortunately, even if it is not so difficult to become your dog's Alpha, many owners do not try to achieve this goal due to superficiality or negligence.

Any dog must follow a leader and learn acceptable social behaviors from him. So, until they are taught these behaviors, they must be considered innocent of what they do.

If they do not have a leader to guide them in what is right and wrong, they have no direction and will act according to their wishes, thus appearing undisciplined.

11.2 How to become an alpha

You must choose an alpha from those who live in your home to guide your dog and be supported in his role by the rest of the family. Your Australian Shepherd puppy will obey and become sociable only if he has an alpha leader to admire and follow.

In addition to being self-confident, the one who will take on this critical role must be charismatic and intelligent. The other family members must never question the rules dictated by the Alpha to accept a specific dog behavior. All family members must behave as if they were inside the pack, following the alpha guide for everything related to your Australian Shepherd. Doing so is essential.

You should never reward your Australian Shepherd's antisocial behavior, and the rules must always be strictly adhered to. Any family member must reside above your dog in the imaginary pecking order. Other people, such as visiting friends and family, will have to help strengthen the protocol of rules established for the education of your dog.

The alpha member of the family will walk through doors, go for walks, and eat and drink before everyone else.

Visiting family and friends must abide by these rules so that humans will stand above your dog. Begin this process with love to build a relationship of trust and affection with your four-legged friend.

The alpha leader must control every situation through the power deriving from mental abilities and not just physical ones. As an alpha, you must guide your Aussie's behavior gently and firmly simultaneously to take the correct direction.

Mindful and caring leadership will allow peaceful and loving coexistence with your dog, whether it is socialization training or obedience training.

11.3 Why does your Australian Shepherd need an alpha?

He may disrespect you and have undesirable behaviors if he does not have guidance. In short, to avoid any misbehavior of your Australian Shepherd, you must become his alpha.

Your Aussie wants to be dominated by you, and if you don't become his alpha, his pack leader, he will assume a position of dominance on his own. As a result, he will have disobedient behavior, combine a series of disasters, and make illogical and untamed decisions, such as destroying the newly bought armchair.

What you need to do, then, is become his undisputed alpha from the very first day your Australian Shepherd enters the house.

CHAPTER 12: The hunting instinct of the Australian Shepherd

In this final chapter, you will find exciting information about herding dogs that will help you better understand the specific characteristics of these types of dogs.

The more you know about your Australian Shepherd, the more educated you will be on how to best understand and train them.

12.1 Fundamental characteristics of shepherd dogs

Sheepdogs, also called working or livestock dogs, were initially bred to work or for herding. However, these dogs carry intense herding instincts from ancient hunting skills. In fact, since the earliest times, humans and dogs began to live and work side by side, relying on each other to survive.

For this reason, humans have begun to use herding dogs to guard pets and to develop other dog breeds to manage and protect flocks and livestock from any threat.

Thus, the guard and sheep dogs began to work together to defend the livestock and keep them safe.

Think of the mountain dogs of the great mountain ranges who take care of guard duties every day and the shepherds who carry out herding duties simultaneously.

Sheepdogs have extraordinary abilities to obey whistles and voice commands and carry out their work independently.

12.2 The sheepdog instincts of the Aussie

Sheepdogs bite, bark, run and have intense eye contact with their animals. Australian Shepherds are famous for their runs on top of sheep to keep them going and for their still, squatting style through which they hypnotize and collect nearly any animal together.

Additionally, Australian Shepherds jump upward to attack cows' necks or approach heels if necessary. The Aussie grazes more upright than other breeds and tends to move towards livestock more quickly.

The Australian Shepherd is intelligent, courageous, independent, and endowed with the stamina and intense energy needed to do his job with diligence and attention. In addition to herding, the Australian Shepherd is often used as a guide dog, therapy dog, or police dog.

Its versatility allows this breed to raise and watch ducks, cattle, geese, goats, and sheep. It can also guard pets, children, and other dogs and, if not tied up, could even herd motor vehicles.

If Australian Shepherds do not have a job but have to play the role of companion animals, due to their instincts, they will have to be trained firmly and be able to carry out the assigned tasks.

This goal can be achieved with satisfaction through physical training, chase games, herding trials, hiking, walking, and brisk walking.

An Australian Shepherd who does not exercise could become aggressive and violent and engage in negative behavior. Therefore, before taking an Australian Shepherd home, you must ensure you can provide them with the required amount of physical and mental exercise. Any sheepdog must go out several times a day and get at least two hours of rigorous training.

There are various types of Australian shepherds at the descent of coat, height, and weight; however, most Australian shepherds fall into the medium-large sizes.

At least since the ninth century, the Australian Shepherd has been watching and breeding ducks, geese, cattle, horses, and sheep, and especially in recent times, it has been used to keep geese and ducks away from airports or golf courses.

The Australian Shepherd tends to be wary of strangers while forming close bonds with his family members. He is an excellent companion animal and enjoys being around humans.

An essential aspect of dealing with from an early age is the bite; you must always supervise your dog in the presence of small children.

When these play and run around, your Aussie, like a sheepdog, will recognize that it is a herd to care for and begin to nibble on their heels. You will notice that they instinctively go around a group of children, behaving like a sheepdog. Their intention is not to hurt, but a bite could cause pain.

With early and continuous socialization, you can fight negative behaviors such as possessiveness, territorialism, aggression, and more.

Australian Shepherds are much happier when they have a goal, and this is because they are an intelligent, active, and work-oriented breed.

Conclusion

Now that you have read this book, you will feel more familiar with this beautiful dog breed. I hope you have enjoyed reading it and feel ready to select and raise your new friend.

If you desire to own a medium-sized dog with a beautiful colored coat and extraordinarily versatile once well trained, the Australian Shepherd is a perfect choice.

Everything you've read so far will help you train your Australian Shepherd. There are many methods, tricks, tools, and little things to deal with your dog. Of course, you will never stop learning, but this is what will amuse you and will bond you more and more to your Australian Shepherd.

During your training experience, you will experience days and times when you think your dog will never learn and become polite and balanced. You will overcome difficult times, and the result will be that you will understand each other with your dog on any level, gaining maximum control over him.

Owning an Australian Shepherd is a big commitment worth making for many reasons.

You need to learn to think like your dog and be patient, just as you have it with yourself and your children. If you can do this, you will have a relationship and a close bond for years.

The company of an Australian Shepherd will bring you joy, love, and friendship like no one else could.

Consult this book often and look for other resources, such as training manuals; hang out with experienced friends who love dogs the same way you can share happy and sad moments. Never stop improving your training skills; remember that your efforts will keep you and your Australian Shepherd pleased for a long time.

The Australian Shepherd is a wise, intelligent dog with great qualities. It is well known for being a protective working-dog towards its owner and family.

The Australian Shepherd has a strong guard instinct and thinks he can constantly manipulate his environment. This breed loves its family beyond measure and tolerates strangers or other people it does not know with education but not with great enthusiasm.

This book will surely be useful on your beautiful journey alongside your Australian Shepherd.

Thanks to this guide, you will have a complete overview of the extraordinary world of the Australian Shepherd.

Made in the USA
Las Vegas, NV
05 November 2023